www.SelfLearnChinese.com

A BOOK FOR BEGINNERS TO LEARN CHINESE CHARACTERS

VOLUME 1

找汉字识字游戏

www.SelfLearnChinese.com

RUYI HUA

华如意

www.SelfLearnChinese.com

PREFACE

Each book in the "Fast Reading Chinese Characters" series contains thousands of simplified Chinese characters (简体中文) organized in the form of puzzles. For each puzzle of 6*6 grid, you have to find a given character (汉字) given right before the puzzle. All puzzles contain multiple similar looking and easily confused characters, helping your brain to distinguish and correctly remember the complex Chinese pictographs. The characters to be found include the Pinyin (拼音) and English (英文) meaning of each of the characters, making the book suitable for HSK all level students. The solution of the puzzles has been provided in the books. By solving these puzzles, you will be able to fast recognize, and remember the Chinese characters in the long-term. The book is suitable for all levels of Mandarin Chinese language students. In particular, the simple and manageable 6*6 size character search puzzles, inclusion of English and pinyin makes the book a perfect choice of the beginners.

©2023 Ruyi Hua

All rights reserved.

CONTENTS

PREFACE 2

CONTENTS 3

CHAPTER 1: TEST (1-10) 4

CHAPTER 2: TEST (11-20) 9

CHAPTER 3: TEST (21-30) 14

CHAPTER 4: TEST (31-40) 19

CHAPTER 5: TEST (41-50) 24

ANSWERS (1-50) 29

CHAPTER 1: TEST (1-10)

1. 景 (Jǐng): View					
饱	旱	稍	灸	春	丕
景	貅	綦	义	六	猷
泌	畚	碜	紧	九	璟
烂	烦	挛	郏	台	殃
瓠	寒	妄	景	鸾	轮
克	任	景	磐	胥	邯

2. 颍 (Yǐng): Name of a river in Henan and Anhui					
郗	旱	稍	灸	春	丕
富	貅	綦	义	六	猷
觚	畚	碜	紧	九	璟
搂	烦	挛	郏	台	殃
夸	寒	妄	景	鸾	轮
念	任	景	磐	胥	邯

3. 孤 (Gū): Orphan

虒	孤	郑	枸	晕	蕨
耦	飧	洗	刹	奋	单
冲	孤	肾	弄	全	熙
窬	起	赛	卜	孤	恳
褊	另	舻	孤	价	犹
殍	颤	恶	孤	孤	蛾

4. 篇 (Piān): A piece of writing

包	隋	祎	喧	缪	反
珊	谐	篇	篇	恶	虤
娴	咸	欨	诈	函	度
阮	逼	豘	篇	果	露
粕	幼	翰	篇	袄	院
弋	形	厥	款	璟	觑

5. 帘 (Lián): Flag on pole over wine house

措	鹉	尔	答	煞	设
雾	舸	尉	帘	众	旦
呼	绺	旎	居	次	宪
浏	割	艰	沓	汩	扎
仙	詹	麽	窥	缜	孽
划	帘	珥	幽	歃	勺

6. 颂 (Sòng): Praise

饕	靓	颂	颂	沙	废
乱	沓	系	环	牟	龋
掉	仿	龇	千	花	端
头	弴	颂	糕	邯	焦
念	家	齿	龅	剜	糜
各	跳	颂	防	粥	聂

7. 蜀 (Shǔ): Shu, a state in the Zhou Dynasty

瓶	累	斛	节	熟	蜀
皱	戈	奚	售	筋	篱
牙	盈	燕	夐	悲	那
蜀	蜀	罂	屡	陔	唇
肛	勒	粘	跄	礼	号
旋	悟	粉	蜀	辘	沏

8. 叩 (Kòu): Knock

尺	痘	少	沔	卵	灭
叩	孩	畿	糟	宕	继
考	吆	午	确	耶	匪
馃	难	责	粮	戏	昇
希	左	霖	汶	弗	释
霈	棕	忽	馄	魈	清

9. 稻 (Dào): Rice					
狒	皈	垃	橘	列	震
憙	鲑	尾	邵	耕	劳
住	耵	渗	酞	影	密
棠	狐	稻	稻	殊	粤
空	稀	厨	裳	髟	稻
唇	绠	蛮	盂	圾	骰

10. 盆 (Pén): Basin					
鉴	蘁	斩	达	颜	奇
畿	骒	浇	胃	盆	戴
犊	钆	佘	蒸	晕	寄
种	爱	裳	应	珥	痹
沁	歁	创	飙	承	占
瞑	浒	疗	酞	匠	盆

CHAPTER 2: TEST (11-20)

11. 觏 (Gòu): Meet					
饼	砝	付	幽	范	奥
利	私	另	翡	番	童
领	覃	站	觏	的	觏
馥	邝	泊	觏	区	忘
弛	觏	众	申	弱	瓢
联	觏	韶	在	卒	壹

12. 瑶 (Yáo): Precious jade					
愫	教	翘	汩	洗	税
忎	踔	邗	分	瑶	厦
瑶	亮	寂	亥	旦	泋
宿	愿	皖	熏	絮	鲑
炊	压	陷	创	毫	底
艨	顽	端	漏	密	蹲

13. 窜 (Cuàn): Flee					
户	鑫	窜	鳎	区	渤
窜	醒	沤	呼	胖	翰
场	活	窜	郯	判	琚
旬	昼	汗	泽	缪	窜
背	差	茂	窜	脏	饺
耵	耙	鸦	碌	虚	甄

14. 耏 (Ér): Beard					
复	豕	烂	妻	陕	郔
嚏	亩	就	耏	陑	轨
靠	畸	汁	矿	税	砈
淼	医	尤	跺	肉	韫
耏	家	至	耏	它	建
耏	即	忒	耧	臭	耏

15. 泽 (Zé): Pool

酶	泽	纂	轻	甸	玄
枯	特	丑	芈	窈	泽
裆	泽	朝	姗	泽	缋
独	泽	狐	供	愦	塞
耶	玉	各	琊	鳌	旧
献	汕	泽	沈	雎	鱿

16. 沆 (Hàng): A vast expanse of water

沆	跑	拳	隶	馁	酬
恐	场	决	浑	酥	舭
弗	杰	狗	沔	艑	沆
匪	骚	砹	翳	皆	的
旎	政	盔	觇	被	皇
龈	夏	域	阶	犍	旭

17. 详 (Xiáng): Detailed					
卒	鲦	瘫	爱	顷	须
奔	盔	吉	泗	绿	汾
圠	详	罟	占	详	参
夒	岘	骭	泅	散	员
照	骁	鹜	煺	鲜	鲊
详	规	仰	尖	釉	飑

18. 狠 (Hěn): Ruthless					
器	狠	仙	瓴	匈	靶
员	醒	沛	殡	霖	虔
量	突	弯	蹚	燕	弈
射	沄	川	压	絮	乿
炮	髂	坡	泄	煦	望
狠	窈	躬	轧	下	萨

19. 祭 (Jì): Hold a memorial ceremony for

要	驶	旧	朗	悸	握
掀	罩	性	乩	冱	箴
巨	觜	识	糖	体	娘
酥	余	祭	饕	江	海
磐	戽	觋	祭	祭	跟
书	宙	祭	奇	那	阮

20. 冽 (Liè): Cold

抓	飐	驷	酽	沿	教
戛	姬	陆	敢	醛	宕
欸	缋	霓	勒	珸	煞
东	邠	犊	冽	冽	冽
陇	晶	冽	靠	冽	怀
绳	弟	论	卡	缤	黜

CHAPTER 3: TEST (21-30)

21. 矿 (Kuàng): Ore deposit					
相	父	校	据	弑	矿
噪	奂	鸿	陲	煾	篁
驳	异	矿	髁	堕	测
屡	鹞	陨	矿	矿	允
耄	班	松	蛛	店	陛
醴	贡	后	天	滑	贡

22. 郜 (Gào): A surname					
治	汗	盆	沱	沟	孔
跺	厨	乞	磊	耿	肌
曾	解	鲍	郜	廊	夜
系	罨	营	乃	燃	沮
醱	饼	阮	炮	炮	胜
杞	倏	登	雯	辜	琶

23. 耶 (Yé): At the end of a question

觐	稣	酎	奔	匍	廷
聪	勹	枯	泠	鲱	只
爵	卦	瓷	髋	号	莹
细	貊	监	之	耶	估
鸪	耶	硒	泖	杰	文
来	耶	攀	颁	即	珥

24. 肉 (Ròu): Meat

壬	潮	鹄	汜	管	肉
洎	沣	饴	舡	烊	卜
肉	皆	旬	相	泯	肉
猴	郓	躺	肉	沁	幽
家	鸭	掀	呎	特	娲
里	疫	旎	鲊	虹	瘌

25. 卷 (Juàn): Volume

技	仇	鳌	脉	卷	楣
卷	棕	底	罗	矶	屏
测	强	症	泝	棠	约
沐	赟	髇	卷	属	卷
斿	齿	殖	盛	协	碾
呼	捂	分	觌	月	坒

26. 煎 (Jiān): Fry in shallow oil

冱	斤	胖	弭	驷	匈
躲	衰	艑	拉	隆	獗
瓯	煎	馥	果	灵	红
戗	町	邲	翊	太	擎
勾	鹰	畜	煎	利	扃
别	黪	聂	亥	朝	百

27. 弊 (Bì): Abuse

旮	陂	爷	罩	号	客
曝	弊	饷	须	癫	弊
笔	皖	裱	没	汍	异
沔	杞	粪	次	正	料
弁	牧	鳔	泮	郁	泞
忠	隈	坷	夸	匈	泾

28. 酣 (Hān): To one's heart's content

娘	莹	爱	掌	治	匝
髋	邸	蚂	娲	沆	丹
景	皆	魁	酣	硫	酣
酣	谦	庶	酣	相	萦
龉	皆	坡	酣	耜	酣
耠	胜	冬	象	搁	炸

29. 邙 (Máng): The name of the mountain, in Henan Province, China

邙	嚏	宓	茹	爱	耆
废	邙	爹	初	亩	料
腰	魑	邙	鲔	邙	郊
洞	邙	邙	策	摹	甘
笨	霸	亮	蠢	瓠	登
尉	弃	或	织	喆	郑

30. 畚 (Běn): A bamboo or wicker scoop

南	繁	赶	半	幽	亥
索	贱	赣	不	畚	尴
乳	攸	畚	海	圾	畚
靶	狩	丫	琭	渗	絮
拉	鹿	议	洞	袜	般
骚	姬	脸	肇	畚	秀

CHAPTER 4: TEST (31-40)

31. 畠 (Tián): Dryland					
銮	阮	泽	沵	腔	戕
局	亡	畠	皑	类	获
螨	汀	少	饼	畠	渣
裕	炮	攻	贬	兴	魁
尽	邻	号	腼	汪	聿
创	既	创	沣	夜	挚

32. 躲 (Duǒ): Hide					
躲	躲	风	耻	斥	痫
教	孚	箱	敌	唇	午
愈	鳌	沁	脊	谦	谤
甙	时	承	沽	卬	甓
昏	孚	盔	经	躲	沟
洑	耍	客	糙	掉	旷

33. 匠 (Jiàng): Craftsman

早	欺	赦	挂	脔	式
汩	贱	匠	罟	匠	隗
顾	邪	身	丢	匠	靳
篇	轻	欤	膈	饴	匠
饲	暇	匠	部	媚	匠
沫	蕨	仁	索	獒	式

34. 翳 (Yì): Slight corneal opacity

挑	我	花	宪	灵	叩
歼	脊	骗	个	丧	约
躬	曦	秃	冯	愿	勺
顾	张	郊	邛	飞	矿
轧	罘	魇	葛	强	豪
碴	攸	寄	备	九	酷

35. 绳 (Shéng): Rope					
潮	毪	鲦	袒	旌	龁
酸	逐	貂	九	烘	特
乐	支	艔	郝	置	闸
皂	父	韶	监	宣	屦
顾	露	耘	久	碴	媛
冷	站	聚	汉	货	卿

36. 是 (Shì): Yes					
赛	滋	庶	刘	旺	屉
是	帛	雍	决	罡	舡
笃	扎	瓠	磐	必	坊
繇	郁	煮	翅	蛊	单
仓	皇	灭	是	价	苗
负	雯	是	鳔	嚏	馇

37. 牙 (Yá): Tooth

相	泠	月	凹	狲	场
馇	砝	暇	盇	牙	巷
光	历	牙	递	朱	倮
薨	灭	邴	焗	包	靓
畚	后	蜃	翡	瓮	泛
将	俏	牙	硅	泌	骱

38. 觏 (Gòu): Meet

糍	馇	邓	背	稻	猜
弨	私	飕	丕	各	恳
弃	觏	觏	觏	夫	思
别	津	巡	猹	忝	饺
瑰	捶	教	黪	赊	磋
番	孩	都	职	甙	璩

39. 罨 (Yǎn): Net for catching birds or fish

炮	婕	员	震	汕	雾
酶	阮	娴	猛	池	旬
筑	罨	赏	罨	衰	需
罨	罨	麽	沨	挈	贪
蒜	盒	员	鲱	估	祜
程	勒	赦	罨	罨	泔

40. 罝 (Jū): Net for catching hare

泪	斌	沙	蚂	齐	瓢
鹛	明	礬	剥	旬	划
孥	馗	聒	罝	荥	殆
豨	赋	割	父	腰	罝
泗	的	蛾	永	鄢	郎
沃	瘟	匆	点	罝	畸

CHAPTER 5: TEST (41-50)

41. 殡 (Bìn): Lay a coffin in a memorial hall					
鞯	珀	寄	量	饰	无
夯	死	釜	定	梵	殡
汀	胱	床	款	恐	通
秸	膀	陬	掌	卧	殡
然	够	符	驰	筑	扈
疢	嚓	魁	酴	故	室

42. 那 (Nè): That					
索	舁	狩	楠	释	庞
砥	狠	鲧	奇	驾	妈
普	那	馆	富	炉	泉
糖	穿	秃	沼	秘	愈
庆	念	那	贱	邹	豀
惋	叛	豹	乖	界	艑

43. 酶 (Méi): Enzyme

刘	肌	阳	皱	乩	牙
疫	乔	恶	上	款	转
号	堕	雷	汁	耨	搂
刺	酶	稼	尽	素	店
好	剃	身	每	蒜	窈
癌	酶	剥	赞	倾	时

44. 婶 (Shěn): Aunt

洞	鹊	泌	顽	跑	骊
登	羿	羿	新	腚	京
殓	吆	犍	紧	犄	冲
和	酱	览	廉	挑	尽
遮	婶	畴	局	旭	桌
死	虢	寺	质	浆	厅

45. 黪 (Cǎn): Dark

疙	瘪	老	恙	飐	裆
耶	惋	海	弊	跪	萌
弍	板	孵	轴	瑰	炒
后	体	涩	邰	臭	炉
佘	粕	敏	芒	鲫	黪
黪	任	汁	焗	盖	粥

46. 卉 (Huì): (various kinds of) grass

粮	号	烊	壶	井	卉
轮	柿	卉	莹	觥	卉
赟	翘	突	恶	旮	鲜
翡	瓯	泅	译	卉	涩
荣	嚏	卉	万	糜	卉
肩	飐	龋	购	甄	霉

47. 凿 (Zuò): Certain					
畋	潮	艰	窕	跳	凿
诈	步	邱	沃	齿	倾
膀	凿	凿	匝	矴	泸
爽	太	凿	泗	贬	壹
疟	民	髋	翘	住	碴
躺	觌	舨	屏	据	迁

48. 臭 (Chòu): Smelly					
提	秴	犀	那	觖	臭
臭	狍	隐	鸣	汁	窕
搂	家	奕	泌	阵	袄
飙	死	龈	臭	乱	饴
耶	仙	甲	宣	刘	形
贱	凌	廉	藻	盏	分

49. 捶 (Chuí): Hammer

獙	黛	觑	秌	鄝	孝
揣	捶	窥	申	宁	捶
捶	捶	灼	趔	乩	黟
茶	炉	窠	枸	宨	赪
占	寻	斋	窠	髌	弌
捶	捶	外	捶	捶	龃

50. 公 (Gōng): Stateowned

褚	腐	靖	宁	兴	陆
穷	鞁	卫	芈	公	孟
公	钐	瓠	公	戴	聘
竖	区	袜	种	跳	公
赣	函	肩	垂	久	饰
垦	整	乐	鲊	腰	将

ANSWERS (1-50)

#1. 景 (3)	#21. 矿 (4)	#41. 殡 (2)
#2. 颖 (1)	#22. 郜 (1)	#42. 那 (2)
#3. 孤 (6)	#23. 耶 (3)	#43. 酶 (2)
#4. 篇 (4)	#24. 肉 (4)	#44. 婶 (1)
#5. 帘 (2)	#25. 卷 (3)	#45. 黪 (2)
#6. 颂 (4)	#26. 煎 (2)	#46. 卉 (6)
#7. 蜀 (4)	#27. 弊 (2)	#47. 凿 (4)
#8. 叩 (1)	#28. 酣 (6)	#48. 臭 (3)
#9. 稻 (3)	#29. 邝 (6)	#49. 捶 (8)
#10. 盆 (2)	#30. 畚 (4)	#50. 公 (4)
#11. 靓 (5)	#31. 畠 (2)	
#12. 瑶 (2)	#32. 躲 (3)	
#13. 窜 (5)	#33. 匠 (6)	
#14. 耏 (5)	#34. 翳 (0)	
#15. 泽 (6)	#35. 绳 (0)	
#16. 沆 (2)	#36. 是 (3)	
#17. 详 (3)	#37. 牙 (3)	
#18. 狠 (2)	#38. 靓 (3)	
#19. 祭 (4)	#39. 罨 (6)	
#20. 冽 (5)	#40. 置 (3)	

www.ingramcontent.com/pod-product-compliance
Lightning Source LLC
LaVergne TN
LVHW062002070526
838199LV00060B/4236